Americana in Miniature

Estelle Ansley Worrell

Photographs by Henry Widick

VAN NOSTRAND REINHOLD COMPANY

NEW YORK   CINCINNATI   TORONTO   LONDON   MELBOURNE

To
Norman

Van Nostrand Reinhold Company Regional Offices:
New York • Cincinnati • Chicago • Millbrae • Dallas

Van Nostrand Reinhold Company International Offices:
London • Toronto • Melbourne

Library of Congress Catalog Card Number 72-9710
ISBN 0-442-29562-6

Designed by Visuality

Published by Van Nostrand Reinhold Company
A Division of Litton Educational Publishing, Inc.
450 West 33rd Street, New York, N.Y. 10001

Published simultaneously in Canada by
Van Nostrand Reinhold Ltd.

1 3 5 7 9 11 13 15 16 14 12 10 8 6 4 2

Preface

This book illustrates American history in an unusual way. To many people, the word illustration means a drawing or painting, but I have chosen the medium of the miniature setting, each of which represents the costumes, furniture, and activities of a particular time in America's past.

Illustrating interiors and costumes presented few problems; I constructed all of the furnishings and dolls shown in this book, using a scale of 2 inches to 1 foot, with the techniques described in my first two books. But illustrating important inventions, historic events, customs, and leisure-time activities was more complicated. For example, when I wanted to show that the steam engine had been invented, or that balloon-flying had became popular, I would have had to construct a scale-model locomotive 5 or 6 feet long, or a huge balloon. Eventually I came upon the idea of representing such events by showing them as the toys of the dolls in the miniatures. I decided that even if particular toys were not being manufactured at a given time, we could assume that at least one clever toymaker or loving relative would have celebrated an important event or development by making a toy to represent it. Thus, the toys I have shown are historically accurate in their design, and may represent an important invention, a toy of the period, or both.

With this problem solved, I knew that I had found a method of illustrating history that had not been explored very much. It also provided the opportunity for using some charming miniatures in my collection that were too small in scale to be incorporated any other way.

Miniature settings allow us to see ourselves in a more detached way than full-size settings do. A decade or event can be seen as a whole, as though (because of the reduced scale) the viewer is far away. A miniature setting, by eliminating unnecessary details, can express the essence of a time or a thing.

Contents

1. Pilgrim Kitchen

KNIVES, WOODEN DISHES

WOOD UTENSILS

In early American homes, a main room with a large fireplace was the dining room, kitchen, and sometimes even the bedroom. The family spent much of its time in this room around the fireplace where the cooking was done. Every member of the family worked — authorities in Massachusetts even directed all girls and boys "to learn the spinning of yarn."

Oriental rugs were used as table covers and wall hangings instead of on the floor. Wooden dishes were used because china dishes were not yet being imported. Plates were just hollowed out pieces of wood, while bowls and dippers were made from gourds. Each person, including young children, had his own knife at meal time. He cut with it and then used it to pick up his food and eat with it! But people used their fingers as much as they used their knives. Early spoons were made of wood and clam shells but were only used for dipping and serving.

Thanksgiving was celebrated every year but not yet on one particular day. Each colony just proclaimed a day of thanks whenever it wanted to. Sometimes the Thanksgiving feast lasted for three days!

Christmas was celebrated by going to church.

FIREPLACE

GIRL SPINNING

2. Early Colonial Children

The Pilgrims dressed in very plain clothing of black, brown, gray, or purple with practically no trimmings at all. Most children's clothes were made of homespun linsey-woolsey (half linen, half wool). The father usually made their shoes while the mother knitted their stockings.

A Massachusetts law required all boys over ten years of age to be trained in shooting bows and arrows. Girls stayed home and helped do the housework; usually only the boys went to school after the first few years.

Some of our early settlers were Dutch, and they brought the custom of making Easter eggs with them as well as games and toys such as dollhouses, dolls (called "babies"), sleds, golf, and ice skating. Early Colonial children played with alphabet blocks too. And they had swings, stilts, tops, and jump rope as we do today. Indian children played similar games and are believed to have been very expert at stilt-walking and cat's cradle. They taught colonists how to make cornhusk dolls.

Storytelling and reading aloud were popular forms of amusement, and books were being read for enjoyment as well as for learning for the first time. The first elementary textbook, *The New England Primer*, was printed in 1691.

The first sporting event on record in America was a kind of football game between a team of Indians and some boys in Boston about 1650. The game was played with an inflated ox bladder, and the teams were barefoot!

NEW ENGLAND PRIMER, ALPHABET BLOCKS

INDIAN CHILD

BOW AND ARROW

EASTER EGGS

CORNHUSK DOLL

3. Early Colonial Interior

Southern settlers wore fancier clothing than the Pilgrims did. Sometimes men curled their hair and sometimes they shaved it all off and wore curly wigs. They wore lace and ribbons on their clothes and carried lace handkerchiefs. Women wore velvet and brocade dresses, hats with plumes, and fur muffs.

The clothes children wore were almost exactly like those worn by grown-ups. Little girls even wore tight corsets, which were probably terribly uncomfortable.

Furniture at this time was not especially comfortable because it was straight and hard. Much of it was just decorated boxes, such as writing and Bible boxes, dough boxes, and dower chests. Later, as people thought of attaching legs, these boxes became desks, cabinets, and chests of drawers; as people constructed chairs and stools wider and wider, they became benches and settees.

MEN'S CLOTHING

PAINTED CHEST

SETTEE

4. Early 18th Century Bedroom

NEEDLEWORK

Men's coats had grown longer and fuller until they were knee-length by the beginning of the 18th century. This style was so popular that it continued for many years. Men sometimes still shaved their heads and wore a long curly wig called a "periwig." They rarely wore their three-cornered hats because they didn't want to muss their hair.

For a short time at the beginning of the 18th century women wore dresses that were fitted in front and full and flowing in back.

The first beds in America were low-post or cupboard beds; canopied beds came into use a little later. Foot stoves were used at home, school, and church to keep warm. At night, bricks or metal bed warmers were used to warm the beds.

Patchwork and crewel embroidery were done by women for bed covers, hangings, and cushions. The art of patchwork was invented by American women who used every bit of handwoven cloth so that nothing was wasted. Young girls were doing needlework items for their homes by the time they were nine years old! The earliest crewel work was just blue, white, and brown.

FOOT STOVE

BED WARMER

5. Colonial Shops

Even though children worked, they were allowed to play more now than a few years before. There are even records that toy shops were opened in some towns. Benjamin Franklin remembered that in 1713 he bought a whistle in a toy shop in Boston.

Public libraries were started and the first *Mother Goose* book was printed in 1719. Other children's books such as *Gulliver's Travels* and *Robinson Crusoe* were published in England.

Mail was being sent as often as once a week now among some of the colonies except when bad weather prevented it.

The first newspaper in the colonies, *The Boston News-Letter,* was started early in the 18th century. The postmaster had been sending so many messages and hearing so much gossip and news that he started sending out letters to his friends to keep them informed and up to date. Then he decided to send his newsletter out regularly and charge for it — thus the newspaper began!

As early as 1723 there were traveling animal acts, acrobats, and puppet shows for people to enjoy. Dancing schools were becoming more and more popular.

TRAVELING PUPPET SHOW

GIRL WITH BOOK

LETTERS AND BOOK ON DESK

6. Mid-18th Century Bedroom

Shortly after the middle of the 18th century men began to powder their hair or their wigs with flour. Women copied them and powdered theirs too. They piled their hair high on top of their heads over a wire frame and kept it stuck there with a mixture of flour and oil! They went for days, or even weeks, without taking it down. Some very stylish ladies wore their hair so high that they had to be careful they didn't snag it on the chandeliers that were popular at the time.

Women, and young girls also, wore beauty patches on their chins, cheeks, or foreheads. Their dresses were worn over side hoops which made them so wide that they often had to turn sideways to go through doorways.

Tea-drinking was extremely popular because tea was being imported from China. The tea kettle and the teaspoon were new to the colonies too, as was the tea table.

Crewel work was still very fashionable for household items and clothing too. Women had learned much about vegetable dyes from the Indians, so many beautiful colors were used now.

TEA TABLE

SPOON RACK WITH TEASPOONS

WIG ON STAND

7. Mid-18th Century Drawing Room

By the 1760s music was popular and Charleston, South Carolina, actually had an orchestra of paid musicians who gave regular concerts.

It was fashionable for people to get together and spend an afternoon or evening of singing or playing music just for enjoyment. Popular instruments were violins, guitars, mandolins, flutes, organs, drums, fifes, and harpsichords.

Theatre was enjoyed too although it was not legal yet. The first performance we know about was given in Williamsburg, Virginia, and Charleston even had a small theatre.

Men and boys dressed in suits of velvet, silk, and brocade, with ruffled shirts, for formal wear, and homespun suits and plain shirts for work and play. They always wore white stockings and a black ribbon to tie back their hair. The coats were split in back.

When new homes were built at this time there was a room added that had not previously been there — the drawing room. Because of the new pastimes and games people needed a place to "withdraw" to after dinner.

CHANDELIER

MAN'S POWDERED HAIR

(PHOTO: HOWARD WOLERY)

MANDOLIN

8. Continental Corpsmen

Several wars between France and England took place over more than seventy years, until 1763, with the two countries fighting for power in the New World. The French eventually lost to the English settlers, who liked their new homes in the colonies so much that they were willing to die defending them if necessary.

Later, when the Revolution started, our Continental army did not have uniforms. The Continental corpsman put together his own uniform from what he already had, as settlers had done earlier. His buckskins or linen clothes were most often used. The winter buckskins were trimmed with fur, the summer linens with fringed linen.

Near the end of the war, uniforms were made in France. They were various shades of blue or brown, depending on which colony the corpsman represented. Actually there were more homemade brown colonial uniforms than blue ones, because brown dyes from nuts and berries were easier to get from the farm or forest than blue dyes.

Each soldier carried a canteen often covered with red wool, a musket with bayonet, a powder horn, a shot pouch, and a tomahawk! All this equipment was hung from two baldrics, or straps, crisscrossed over the back and chest, and from a red wool blanket roll.

BACK VIEW OF CORPSMAN WITH BLANKET ROLL, CANTEEN, SWORD

POWDER HORN, TOMAHAWK, MUSKET

9. British Soldier (Redcoat), American Revolution

The British soldiers' uniforms were made the same way, but were usually red with white or black trim; therefore the soldiers were called Redcoats. The British uniforms too were made in France, which explains why they were made the same way. Officers usually wore their coats fastened in a double-breasted style.

The first person killed in the Revolution was a young boy! It happened in one of the early riots, or skirmishes, in Boston in 1770. Young boys took part in the Boston Tea Party in 1773 too.

Most all young boys carried their own knives, which they used for many practical things concerning work, hunting, and fishing. But knives were used for fun too — for making tops, hoops, whistles, bows and arrows, and play guns. Boys were sometimes scolded for wasting so much time whittling.

BRITISH REDCOAT

10. Late 18th Century Children

Children played many games that are still played today, such as marbles, blind man's bluff, hopscotch, baseball, and leapfrog. They flew kites, went swimming, fished with bamboo poles, played cards, and had dolls. Dolls were now called dolls instead of babies. There was a new toy that children were just beginning to enjoy — the lead pencil! It was not yet used in schools.

Some well-to-do families gave presents to children at Christmas at this time even though it was not commonly done yet. Toys were advertised in the newsletters, as were children's books.

At Easter time eggs were dyed in a thick red dye and then scratched with a pin to make designs. Young men and ladies gave these decorated eggs as gifts. Children played a game with theirs; each child would hold an egg in his hand and hit it against the egg in a rival's hand. The person whose egg cracked had to give it to the other person whose egg remained whole.

LEAD PENCILS

QUEEN ANNE DOLL

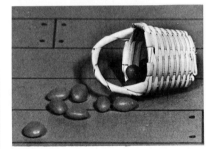

EASTER EGGS

PLAYING CARDS

23

11. Late 18th Century Drawing Room

In 1785 an American doctor accompanied a French balloonist across the English Channel. A few years later an aeronaut made the first balloon ascension in America, and young boys enjoyed playing aeronauts because of this. There was so much interest in balloon-flying, in fact, that a balloon almanac was published.

Sailing ships were returning regularly from China and India with many exciting items. One sea captain brought back a small crate of firecrackers, which he playfully demonstrated for his friends on the Fourth of July!

Clothing was softer and more comfortable as a more natural style gained favor. Women and girls used less powder on their hair, which made it a "mouse" color instead of white, and let it hang down long in back.

Needlepoint was used for rugs, wall hangings, upholstery, and even bed covers. When silver was owned it was displayed where everyone could see it, although pewter was often used instead in smaller homes. Paul Revere made much beautiful silver, but did you know that he also made teething rings, rattles, and whistles for children? Clocks, vases, and figurines were popular accessories.

Although theatre still was not legal, George Washington had several plays given during his inauguration. The laws against theatre were finally abolished in 1793.

SILVER PIECES (PHOTO: HOWARD WOLERY)

BALLOON ALMANAC, EYEGLASSES

WALL CLOCK FIGURINE BALLOON, SAILING SHIP

THEATRE PLAYBILL VASE

12. Early 19th Century Parlor

CRYSTAL CHANDELIER

BICORNE HAT

FRENCH CHAIR

A few years after the Revolution in America, France had her own revolution. The purchase of the Louisiana Territory from France in 1803 made many Frenchmen into U.S. citizens. When the Louisiana Territory was added, the United States more than doubled in size! All this helped to focus attention on France and French fashions.

Some of the ancient ruins of Rome and Greece were excavated about this time, and the drapery and clothing on the statues served as inspiration for French styles. Americans then copied the French styles. Women wore high-waisted, close-fitting dresses of soft material which they actually dampened, even in winter, to make them cling to their bodies like the drapery of the statues! Some people considered these fashions scandalous.

During this period men began wearing long trousers instead of knee breeches. The popular coat of the period was similar to the formal tailcoats worn by men today. Men wore their hair cut short, with very long sideburns. The bicorne, or two-cornered hat, replaced the tricorne or three-cornered hat that had been fashionable for a hundred years.

Wallpaper murals and furniture as well as clothes were being imported and copied from France. Some of this French furniture was bought for the White House, which was built at this time.

13. Early 19th Century Children

In the early 1800s, the American Philosophical Society financed the excavation of the bones of a mastodon (a prehistoric elephant-like mammal) in New York, the first steamship was afloat, the first locomotive was running, and Thomas Jefferson introduced vanilla ice cream to Americans!

Children's clothing was made softer and looser-fitting than before and, as a result, was more comfortable. Little girls no longer had to wear corsets, but boys still wore dresses until they were six or even eight years old! Young girls wore lace-trimmed pantalets and large bonnets with their high-waisted dresses.

Clothing for all ages was more comfortable now because the tape measure had been invented, and tailors and dressmakers were able to make better fitting clothes.

The early 19th-century furniture styles, which were inspired by ancient history, were known as Federal and Empire.

Rocking horses were favorite toys along with wooden dolls, jumping jacks, toy locomotives, boats, and tea sets.

VANILLA ICE CREAM

ROCKING HORSE, TOY STEAM ENGINE

WOODEN DOLL

14. Sailor, 1812 to 1820

CHINA DISHES, FORKS

In the War of 1812, in which the United States Navy fought against the British Navy, naval uniforms were first used. Until this time, seagoing men wore army clothes or their regular clothes. Officers wore dark suits that were much like their formal dress suits. The regular sailors wore white middies with blue trim, striped shirts underneath, bell-bottom trousers, black sailor hats, and flat-heeled slippers, sometimes with bows on the toes. It was on a ship in this war that "The Star Spangled Banner" was written, and a new flag with fifteen stars was made.

It was about this time that shoes were made to fit the right and left feet for the first time since the days of ancient Greece. For centuries people had worn shoes that were shaped the same for both feet when new.

Women's dresses now had full skirts a few inches off the floor. When they walked, the skirts swayed like bells. They wore flat-heeled shoes like those worn by men.

China dishes, silver spoons, and four-pronged forks were so popular that the formal dining room came to be considered a necessary part of every fine home.

SAILOR UNIFORM

RIGHT AND LEFT SHOES

15. Early Theatre Exterior

Parents started dressing little boys in sailor suits, probably because of the recent great naval battles.

Now that theatre was legal, there was much interest not only in seeing plays but in acting in them too. America's first community theatre group was formed in Cincinnati, and they built a small theatre. Someone even thought of giving a theatre performance especially for children about this time; this was the beginning also of youth theatre, sometimes called educational theatre.

Puppetry was still considered mainly adult entertainment but puppet show posters were beginning to say, "Bring the Children."

Baseball, a form of the English game of cricket, had been considered a game for children in the 18th century. Now in the early 19th century it was becoming a sport for adults as well.

The first gold rush in the United States occured when gold was discovered in Georgia in the 1820s!

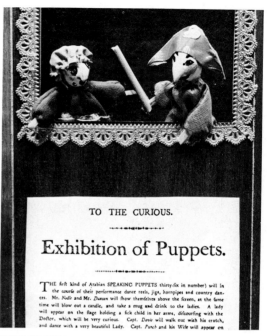

PUNCH AND JUDY

PUPPET SHOW POSTER, 1828

ACTORS JUNIUS B. BOOTH AND EDMUND KEAN, 1820s

16. Early Art, Science, and History Museum

Men wore their hair short now but their sideburns grew so long they became cheek whiskers. They wore top hats over their curled hair.

Women's dresses became fuller around the hems, and the sleeves grew larger and larger until by the 1830s the huge sleeves were wired or stuffed to make them stay out. Shawls and stoles were extremely popular.

The art of ballet was started in France and Italy and then spread to Russia and finally the United States. The costumes and hairdos of ballet were popular styles of the time and are still used today by ballerinas.

The first science, history, and art museums in America were started early in the 19th century. Prehistoric skeletons and stuffed birds and reptiles were displayed along with paintings and sculpture, while puppet shows and other amusements were performed there.

The Peale family, who started America's first public museum (later the Philadelphia Museum), even had a small steam engine with two cars for visitors to ride — our first miniature railroad!

MINIATURE TRAIN POSTER

STOLE AND MUFF

CHEEK WHISKERS, CURLY HAIR

MUSEUM POSTER

35

17. Mexican War Uniform

By 1848, when the war with Mexico ended, the United States for the first time reached from the Atlantic to the Pacific Ocean. The territories of Texas, New Mexico, and California had been added to the United States.

Patriotic emblems and motifs, especially the eagle, were found everywhere. Americans seemed to be bursting with pride in being American!

Toy soldiers became extremely popular after the war, and to this day many are still made wearing the same uniform that soldiers wore in the mid-19th century.

Before mid-century much of the nation had public school systems, but many people still thought that things like music and art should not be taught in schools. By now some colleges were beginning to admit women students for the first time, and a few were admitting black students too. These students could read books that were written by Americans and published in America as new publishing companies were started.

Women were wearing a style that had been popular during the Middle Ages, the princess dress. This dress was different because it had no waist seam — the shaped pieces reached from the shoulder to the hem.

Americans were exchanging Christmas cards that they usually made themselves, and the expression "Merry Christmas and Happy New Year" was first used in newspaper advertisements in the late forties.

Mail was being delivered regularly by stagecoach or boat and another way too — one aeronaut believed that mail could be carried in the air! He proved it could be done by carrying mail in his balloon flights in 1849.

GIRL COLLEGE STUDENT, BOOK

MAIL-STAGE ANNOUNCEMENT, EARLY 19TH CENTURY

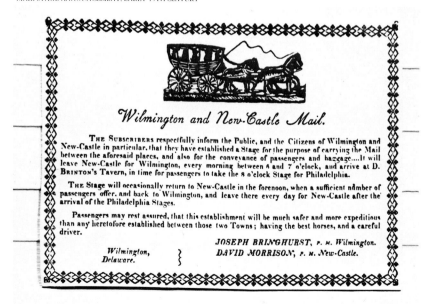

Wilmington and New-Castle Mail.

THE SUBSCRIBERS respectfully inform the Public, and the Citizens of Wilmington and New-Castle in particular, that they have established a Stage for the purpose of carrying the Mail between the aforesaid places, and also for the conveyance of passengers and baggage....It will leave New-Castle for Wilmington, every morning between 6 and 7 o'clock, and arrive at D. BRINTON's Tavern, in time for passengers to take the 8 o'clock Stage for Philadelphia.

THE Stage will occasionally return to New-Castle in the forenoon, when a sufficient number of passengers offer, and back to Wilmington, and leave there every day for New-Castle after the arrival of the Philadelphia Stages.

Passengers may rest assured, that this establishment will be much safer and more expeditious than any heretofore established between those two Towns; having the best horses, and a careful driver.

JOSEPH BRINGHURST, P. M. Wilmington.
DAVID MORRISON, P. M. New-Castle.

Wilmington, Delaware.

18. Mid-19th Century Fashion Shop

In the middle of the 19th century the sewing machine was invented, and cotton and wool production was then industrialized. Now women could sew yards and yards of ruffles, full skirts, and petticoats. Skirts were all the way down to the floor again because all those long seams could be done so quickly with the wonderful new machine. Some skirts were as much as ten yards around the hem! Not only were ruffles popular, but so were embroidery, lace, tassels, braid, fringes, puffs, and swags.

When the paper-pattern business was started in New York, the demand for dress patterns was fantastic. One company claimed to have sold 50,000 of one popular design. Women by the thousands bought patterns for the latest fashions and made dresses for themselves. At last we had reached an age when personal taste and ingenuity determined how we looked, not occupation or class!

Fashion magazines were started too, and included instructions for children's as well as ladies' clothing. Little girls wore starched smocks to protect their fancy dresses.

FASHION MAGAZINES, IRON, WRAPPING PAPER

TAPE MEASURE

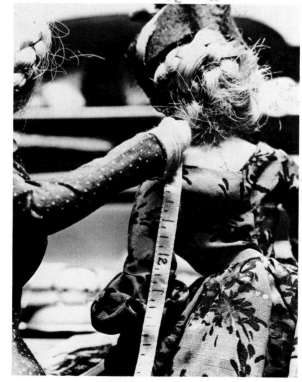

STARCHED SMOCK, PAPER DOLLS

19. Christmas, Mid-19th Century

Young girls were also interested in fashion and the first American commercial paper dolls were published. These early paper dolls and their costumes were based on famous ballerinas, opera singers, historical figures such as Queen Isabella of Spain and characters from current literature, such as Topsy and Little Eva from *Uncle Tom's Cabin*.

It was about this time that the decorated tree became a traditional symbol of Christmas in America. Queen Victoria and Prince Albert (who was German) had been decorating a tree in England, and Americans liked the idea so much that we started doing it here too.

By mid-century it was the custom to give gifts at Christmas time, and children received many toys and presents. Steamboats, locomotives, carriages, pull toys, dollhouses, dolls, soldiers, and rocking horses were popular with boys and girls.

Queen Victoria, who had nine children, also insured the popularity of another new idea, the pram or baby carriage. The bicycle was invented too — it seems that people of *all* ages were traveling someplace now! The first bicycles were experimental, being made of iron and even wood in some cases.

TOY SOLDIERS

PAPER DOLLS

20. Confederate Soldier, Civil War

During the Civil War most Southern mills were shut down, and women had to weave their own cloth and use homemade dyes. They eventually resorted to making garments out of draperies, sheets, old clothes, and even rugs and mattress-ticking. They wore bonnets from wheat and oat straw and bits and scraps of fabric. They trimmed them with berries, flowers, leaves, and even the curled shavings from cow's horns!

For shoes, they tanned their own leather. The hides used were from any and all animals, from sheep to horses. Sometimes they even cut up old saddles, belts, or trunks for leather for the shoe soles.

Confederate uniforms were gray with gold buttons. The stand-up collar and cuffs were blue for infantry, yellow for cavalry, and red for artillery. Officer's dress uniforms had gold braid designs on the sleeves.

As the war grew worse, women had to make uniforms for the Confederate soldiers as well as their own clothes. Most plantations still had old spinning and weaving equipment in the attics. This was brought down, and the older women taught the younger ones how to use it. The amount of cloth they turned out has amazed many historians. Some groups outfitted whole companies of soldiers in homespun, home-dyed, and hand-woven uniforms, which were often brown instead of gray.

CONFEDERATE OFFICER

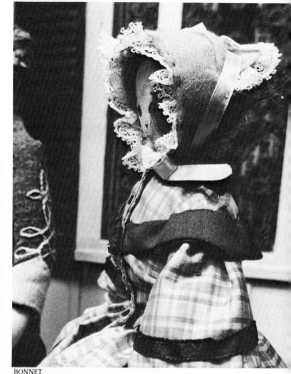

BONNET
CIVIL WAR RECRUITMENT POSTER

21. Union Soldier, Civil War

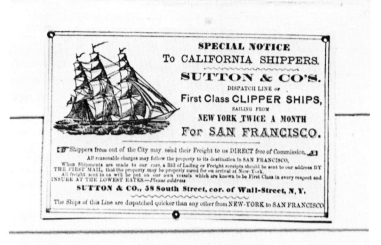

The dark blue Union army uniforms were almost exactly the same as the Confederate ones. Both armies used double-breasted coats for high-ranking officers and single-breasted ones for regular soldiers and lower-ranking officers.

Photography, the telegraph, and postage stamps had been invented and put into use by this time. Gold had been discovered in California, and many people were moving west in hope of striking it rich. They were traveling by wagon or by sailing ship.

Probably the first toy factory in the United States was started in Massachusetts after the Civil War, and toy stores opened in every city. You could buy a pencil with a new invention — the eraser.

One favorite toy was the "zoetrope." This was a drumlike contraption on a stand which had a series of pictures on the inside showing a person in various stages of some action. When the drum was whirled around, the pictures, viewed through slots, appeared to move, as in our modern-day animated movies. This toy and several other similar optical toys were a very early form of motion pictures.

SAILING SHIP NOTICE

EARLY PHOTOGRAPH

ZOETROPE TOY

22. American Music, African Influence

The American folk song and the Negro spiritual developed during mid-century and became a part of our culture.

The guitar had been around since the days of early Egypt and had been played in America during the 18th century, but it was the West Africans who made it popular.

A German musician from Boston who gave a concert in Charleston happened to hear a group of black people singing to the African "bania" (the banjo) and the guitar. He went home and composed the first minstrel song.

The minstrel shows (at first given by black musicians, later by whites impersonating blacks) became one of the most popular forms of musical entertainment in American history. The minstrel started in the forties and by 1860 there were 150 minstrel troups touring America and other parts of the world. The origins of the music were definitely African and would have a strong influence upon American popular music for more than a century.

GUITAR

BANJO

23. American Music, Elizabethan Influence

Rocking chairs were so popular that almost every home had at least one. The rocking chair and also the front porch are still popular today. The bureau or dresser was introduced at this time, and it usually matched a large carved bed. It too is still an important piece of furniture in our homes.

Immigrants from Scotland and Ireland, who settled in the mountains that stretch from Pennsylvania to Georgia during the last part of the 18th century and the first part of the 19th century, added another element to the American sound. They brought their Elizabethan hymns and ballads, which told of love, tragic heroes, and everyday problems and work. They also brought reels and foot-thumping jigs. Their instruments were the dulcimer, guitar, fiddle, bagpipe, and eventually the banjo.

The Scandinavian and French lumberjacks of the northern areas added their own work songs to this gradual mixing of American music.

Although it was not understood at the time, the various forms of American folk or popular music were blending and would eventually become, in the 20th century, one of the things that America is best known for all over the world.

ROCKING CHAIR
BUREAU OR DRESSER

FOLK GUITAR
DULCIMER

24. American Cowboy

The first telephone was installed in the White House in 1878, but it would be several years more before the average home would include one.

As more and more people went west, the cowboy style evolved in the 1870s, 1880s, and 1890s.

The first cowboys were Spanish and Mexican vaqueros who wore work outfits of canvas and leather. Their canvas or denim jackets were at first natural or brown but eventually became the blue denims we know today. Sometimes they painted their denim coats to make them become stiff windbreakers. With these coats they wore vests and chaps of leather. In winter the chaps were often made of bear, pony, or sheep skin.

When working in the dust they pulled neckerchiefs up over their noses and mouths and smeared soot grease under their eyes to cut down on glare, as our football players do today.

When he went into town, the cowboy often wore a fancy vest and a suit jacket. The large wide-brimmed cowboy hat was worn in warm weather, while a fur hat was worn in winter with a fur vest. Sometimes the brim was as much as four inches wide, with a crown seven inches high! The Texans wore their hats flat on top; cowboys farther north preferred rounded crowns.

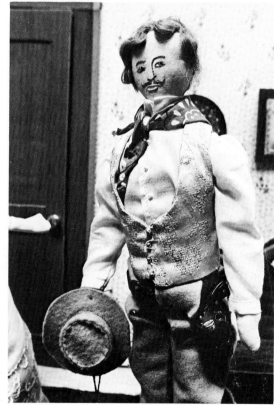

COWBOY NECKERCHIEF, VEST, HAT

EARLY TELEPHONE

COWBOY HAT

25. U.S. Cavalryman, Cowboy

RAILROAD POSTER

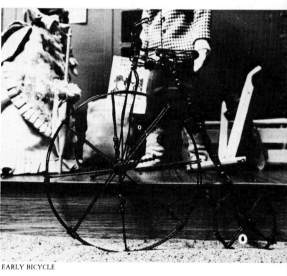
EARLY BICYCLE

Six regiments of U.S. Cavalry helped keep the West open to settlers moving across country to settle on government lands during the Indian wars. Two of these regiments, the famous Ninth and Tenth, were made up of black men and were known as "Buffalo Soldiers." The Indians gave them this name because of the color of their skin and, more importantly, as a compliment to the quality of their fighting.

As the settlers moved west the guitar and ballad went with them. When merged with the Spanish music of the Southwest, it became the American cowboy sound, and still another element was added to American popular music:

Young boys spent a great deal of time with Wild West guns playing cowboys and Indians. There was also interest in roller skating. Crude roller skates had been in existence for several hundred years but now skating was becoming a fad.

Bicycles were creating interest too, even though they were uncomfortable, difficult to ride, and unsafe because they had no brakes. Only men could ride the tall bikes of the 1870s.

The first transcontinental railroad was completed in 1869, when two railroad lines were joined with a golden spike in Utah.

"WANTED" POSTER

26. General Store

ROLLER SKATES

CASH REGISTER

There were factories to make just about everything now, and more and more stores to sell things. There was so much for sale, and people bought so much, that every available space in their homes was filled with something or other.

One thing available was printed Christmas cards. Although people had been exchanging greetings at Christmas for several years, this was the first time you could buy them, even printed in color.

The paper bag had also been invented some years before but had not been commonly used. Now it was being put to good use.

Children had more toys than they had ever had before, and play and leisure were no longer considered sinful. Grown-ups engaged in play too. Bike-riding was growing more popular with the men, and both men and women were enjoying a nationwide craze for roller skating. Roller rinks were being built in most every town so children could skate in the afternoons and grown-ups in the evenings.

The cash register was invented in 1879 and was put to practical use by the eighties. The typewriter was invented too, and was creating many new jobs for women, who were called "type writers."

Clothing was complex and elaborate like everything else. It was not uncommon for ladies' dresses to be made of several different fabrics and trimmings at once. Little girls wore dresses with bustles and fancy trim like their mothers.

CHRISTMAS CARDS AND VALENTINES

PAPER BAG

27. 1880s Interior

In 1884 a man decided to go around the world on his tall bicycle, and he did it — it took him two years! It seems somebody was always going around the world in something or other during this period. People wanted to roll, float, or fly — and at faster and faster speeds.

Men had been wearing the sack coat since just before the Civil War and by the eighties were wearing it for all informal occasions. The sack coat is one that has no waist seam because it is cut in one piece from shoulder to hem. This is basically the same suit coat still worn by men today. About this time laced-up shoes took the place of boots for most occasions. Mustaches were popular, and men oiled their hair with oil from Macassar. Little fancy napkin-like covers were used on chair backs to protect them from this oil. They were called "antimacassars."

Art appreciation became a popular subject, and people bought paintings, sculpture, and art objects in America and Europe. Collecting antique furniture was a hobby (as it still is) of many American wives. Lighter wallpapers and woodwork were gaining popularity.

Both the light bulb and the phonograph had been invented by now and America witnessed its first craze for popular music. By 1900 more than 150,000 phonographs and 3,000,000 records would be bought and enjoyed. Serious music was flourishing during this period too, and a number of symphonies and conservatories were established around the nation.

MUSTACHE, SACK COAT

ANTIQUE FRAMES AND CLOCK

ANTIMACASSAR

28. 1890s American Sports

The automobile was invented, we had our first skyscraper, and newspapers had added something new for the children (and adults too): the comics. You could go for a walk or a ride at night now because many cities had electric street lights for the first time.

In the 1890s skirts were full at the hem but shorter, and the bustle was completely gone. Sleeves were huge and necks were high. One of the reasons for the new gored skirt (fitted at the hips, full at the hem) was that women were engaging actively in sports. Sports or physical education was beginning to be taught in girls' schools, and this skirt could be worn while riding a bicycle, playing tennis, or sailing.

Basketball was invented by an American college professor. It was called basketball because he used real bushel baskets and a soccer ball. Someone had to sit above the baskets and retrieve the good shots until the professor thought of making holes in the baskets!

Figure skating and volley ball also originated in America about this time. Ice skating was centuries old but the sport of figure skating was invented by an American who was ridiculed at first. The idea of combining ballet with ice skating seemed strange to most people until the man went to Finland and opened a school that was immediately successful.

The bicycle now had rubber tires, pedals, and brakes, and was safe enough and small enough for ladies and even children to ride. It was estimated that ten million Americans were riding bicycles.

FIGURE SKATES

SAFETY BICYCLE

GORED SKIRT, TENNIS RACQUET

BASKETBALL AND BASKET

29. 1890s Interior

Toward the end of the century cream and white walls and light floors were being tried by the more daringly modern people, although it would be several more years before the artistic revolution would change the way the average American home looked.

The first electric lights were installed in the White House in 1891, and other homes across the nation were acquiring them too.

Almost every metropolitan city in the country now had at least a small museum, and there was more and more interest in attending theatrical performances. Between 1880 and 1890 the number of actors in the U.S. increased from 5,000 to 15,000.

The railroads had helped theatre because now actors and theatre companies could travel all around the country on tours. The circus was traveling around the country too and was a very popular form of entertainment.

All this interest in theatre was reflected in toys such as miniature toy theatres and puppet theatres, which were enjoyed by both children and adults.

Doll companies were now making boy dolls, nothing like the masculine dolls of today, but boys in fancy dress at least. Dollhouses were a favorite toy, and every child had a variety of toys with wheels.

STRING PUPPET, TRICYCLE

LIGHT BULB, TIFFANY LAMP

DOLLHOUSE, FURNITURE, TOY TRAIN

30. 1900 to 1910 Kitchen

Homes in the cities had indoor plumbing by the early 1900s, and one in every forty Americans had a telephone.

The Wright brothers made their first flight in their motor-driven flying machine in 1903.

The first movie telling a continuous story was made, and going to the movies became the newest pastime to sweep the country.

We were already becoming interested in ecology because President Teddy Roosevelt set aside the first wildlife refuges in the U.S. There was so much interest, in fact, that a new toy was designed for the children called "Teddy's bear."

In 1908 the Olympics included figure skating for the first time. The same basic movements are still used today.

In the early 1900s the bell-shaped skirt was worn. This skirt was gored but not as full as during the 1890s. Women wore their hair in a pompadour.

Little girls wore long-waisted dresses and large bows in their hair. The side part became popular and some little girls were beginning to wear their hair shorter than before, instead of in long curls. The Raggedy Ann doll was another popular new toy.

A new fad was sweeping the nation — chewing gum! The ice cream cone was invented, so ice cream could be eaten at almost any place or time.

Immigrants were coming to America from many countries and bringing new ideas and customs with them.

Just before the First World War women's clothing became shorter and plainer and much like the clothing worn today. Men's clothing also looked like the clothing of today by this time.

Someday the clothing you are wearing right now and the furniture in your house will tell historians something about you and the life you lead. Look at an old photograph of yourself and see how much your clothes tell about where you were or what you were doing that day. When you visit a museum and look at the old clothing worn by people long ago, think about these people and what it must have been like to wear those clothes, live in homes like theirs, and do the same things they did.

RAGGEDY ANN DOLL

TEDDY BEAR

FLYING MACHINE

TELEPHONE

TOY LOCOMOTIVE
EARLY TOY AUTOMOBILES

Acknowledgments

The furniture and dolls shown in this book are handmade, in the way described in my first two books. But the miniatures have come to me in many ways, mostly through the efforts of my family and friends.

The miniatures came from Mexico, Japan, Switzerland, Venezuela, Germany, and many other places throughout the world because my husband Norman, my daughters Anne and Elizabeth, friends such as Dorothy and Tex Ritter, Tom Tichenor, Louise Metzger, and Helen Overton have brought them to me.

How nice to be remembered by a friend traveling, and how nice to be remembered too when an old miniature from someone's childhood turns up! Mabel Love, Betty Everett, and Merrill Everett Ansley have shared some of their beloved old toys with me. Shannon Ansley and Magge Head Kane lent me prized miniatures from their own valuable collections for as long as I needed them.

Sometimes friends such as Peg Lucas, Louise Moss Ansley, and Louise Metzger have made things especially for my collection. For example, Peg Lucas made the Tiffany chandelier from ancient glass fragments that she collected on the desert while in Arabia.

And the children, how can I ever tell them how much I appreciate the things they have done for me! Beth did such beautiful crewel work, Anne made stacks of hat boxes, Clare made the 1890s boy's suit (she learned to sew only weeks before), and all three girls made bonnets, purses, and other items. My husband Norman assembled the covered wagon for me, and our son, Sterling, only seven years old, spent hours brushing antiquing glaze on it so it would be ready the next morning when Hank Widick came to photograph it. His sons Hank and Marc lent me their beautiful western saddles and Edward, Brenda, and Ann Battersby, our neighbors, have often brought me tiny gifts.

Each time it happens it's a beautiful moment for me. It means someone thought of me and wanted to share in the making of this book in some way. Writing a book is hard work but at the same time a beautiful experience. This book, more than the others I have done, has had a kind of magic about it from the very beginning when Jean Koefoed encouraged me to do it. I've re-established old and dear friendships and met some of the most exciting new friends I've ever had, and my life is richer because of it!

One very dear friend of many years, Duncan Everett, passed away while I was working on this book. How I miss his special talent for appearing at my door just when I needed someone to talk to!

So many other friends did things for me. Howard Wolery, Ann Hill, Kent Cathcart, Budd Bishop, Bill Colsher, Sara Andrews, Barbara Harkins, Virginia Denny, and my parents Viola and Sterling Ansley were there with just the right thing when I needed it.

Thank you also to Clara Hieronymus, Leila Phillips, Barbara Moore, Lin Folk, Alice Fullbright, and Teddy Bart for always being willing to help me tell people about my books. And to those people who had confidence in me before I had confidence in myself, Sarah Hill, George and Catherine Dutch, Chris Tibbot, Flora Gill Jacobs, Ray Spilman, John Stover, and Gordon Holl.

Thank you each and every one, I love you all!

Estelle Ansley Worrell